ASCENSION TH

KUHL HOUSE POETS
edited by Mark Levine

ASCENSION THEORY

Poems by

CHRISTOPHER BOLIN

UNIVERSITY OF IOWA PRESS
Iowa City

University of Iowa Press, Iowa City 52242
Copyright © 2013 by Christopher Bolin
www.uiowapress.org
Printed in the United States of America

Design by Barbara Haines

The University of Iowa Press is a member of Green Press Initiative and is committed to preserving natural resources.

Printed on acid-free paper

LCCN: 2013934853
ISBN-13: 978-1-60938-195-0
ISBN-10: 1-60938-195-5

For Kristin, for Finn

Acknowledgments

Grateful acknowledgment is made to the editors of the publications in which the following poems appeared: "Moss in the Shape of Boards" and "Snow Bridge" in *VOLT*; "Cartographer's Mood" and "Census" in *jubilat*; "Updraft" in *1913: A Journal of Forms*; "View" and "Annapolis" in *Post Road*; "New Year" in *Cura*; "Equation for Cresting" in *Lana Turner*.

Thank you to the James A. Michener Foundation and the MacDowell Colony for generous fellowships that aided in the completion of this manuscript. Thank you to Kristin, to Finn, and to my family, for their unwavering support. And, special thanks to Mark Levine for his guidance in bringing this book into the world.

Contents

ASCENSION THEORY

Equation for Cresting

This is the world's reenactment of today,
and of this moment,

    and of continuing on—with its satellite imaging of scattering birds
obscuring our faces—

    and this is the world's reenactment of its percentages:
of the constant shifting of the satellites
and the constant scattering of the birds and the likelihood

that we will be seen;
and this is the reenactment of someone choosing your face

to remember—and of your growing flushed or turning, slightly,
toward a window
with a red shade;

and of the birds' shapes appearing through its fabric—which is
the reenactment

of our traverse
of the capital

      with the flags of thin material gaining symbols in the wind.

Updraft

There are three commas, in this description, of the crown of thorns, and finally a spot of blood.
There are three commas, in this description, which cannot be gotten out, or driven further in.
There are three commas, in this description, and you can see how they bend, when they're struck.
There are three commas, in this description, though only the third, shifted with the crown.
There were three commas, in this description, until another spot of blood fell above the last;
(we must not forget that he is here); that it makes the commas looser, to strike the last,
that he is growing weaker; he is; bleeding out; how it; unfolds; is still beyond our control.
There are three commas, in this description, which bring the body into language, and keep it there.
There are three commas, in this description, which pin these words, to the sheet below.
If we carried his body; if we carried his body in this sheet; (we must not forget that he is here);
what would we ask him; *if the commas were placed, where they could be pulled, what would he have done;*
and, if he turns his head to answer, there will be three commas, in the description of the wound;
and if he turns his head to answer, and the thorns should catch here, who will help him
turn it back, there will be three commas, in the description, of their injured hand.

And Swung Them

Some winters,

I break the jars

from the homestead

not against the walls,

as you might

imagine.

Such a delicate thing:

your son

thinking of apples

as you throw him

in the air;

the horse running

with a rock

in its feedbag.

Annapolis

The midshipmen may be fine
pairing off, in the spray;

each spring,

the flowering trees
make note of their disunities;

the constellations are formed

by projection,
and these shapes (your shoulders)

are coupled

with myth—where the heroes
hail the passersby,

and the passersby are speechless,

and these are notations
to their silence.

Snow Bridge

We laid her on the driftwood pack

and watched its uneven break
sawing against the horizon.

How did you protect her?
The willows woven into the basket were budding.

(I pictured her feet against the ambulance doors
each time they stopped.

I ran through the yard, to wean the hounds
from their mother.)

As we climbed the mountain pass
we lost our switches in the snow,

and the gently arcing trail of a hare,
copied in the pattern of the lace.

We were walking through the snow
to clean the hobbles

which were bent, as if to run.
She left

a needle, glinting from the cross-stitch:
a silo for the grain;

bare fields
in the cross-stitch, winter scene;

and these are
the stitches left by a golden larch

on the forest floor.
How did you know it would end?

I watched
trees mending the sky in the wind

(using her hair as thread).

The Tally

We found only the glass from their goggles

and their crampons buried like traps
beside her numb feet;

faint scratches
on his canvas pants
where he put the paper to his knee.

Then someone slipped into the rescue party.

We noticed an accent in our impersonations
of each other, and grew quiet.

In every impersonation he was angry.

In one, he felled a tree.
And the impersonator, chopping with her hand at the base of a pine

cut her palm.
In another, he asked who had untied the rope
and the impersonator stumbled away from the fire

laughing, we said in the morning, laughing

when we found three, red packs
hung in the trees

spinning.

Footfalls

On the tundra

caribou are dragged
further and

further

to fuel,
to stacks of shuttled wood

burned

out of sequence (leaving

nodes
in every direction

for sensing

the second coming) leaving

early snow
cresting

over the unspent wood: and this
inland

wave carrying

nothing toward them and
nothing

away.

Snow Falling on Scales

This meditation is about appearing without motes between us:
it is practice for presenting oneself to God;

    part of this meditation is the failure of the dog to settle; and your failure to
secure the door;

in truth, part of this meditation is about your failure to remove your shoes
and the failure of the echoes of your steps;

        part of this meditation is about not planting a garden—and
        about not planting a garden, *together*;

part of this meditation is about the beast of burden: about warming its ring
with its breath;

        in truth, its nose was pierced in a meditation, on the boy
who inherited the field: on how the ox had come with the field and no one knew

its commands;
on how a guess turned it left and kept it circling; part of this meditation is about

naming the boy—
and treating his arm;

and part of this meditation is about slowing the circling of the beast.

Remnants of Ice-shelves

Weather-kites
        never reaching the ceiling of the glare:

the expanding fissures
un-spooling their string:

their presence briefly changing
              the properties of things: powdered gloves

deepening a painting's snow—or these downdrafts

        matting fur—

or our songs pulling songs from the Swedes
whose encampments

come nearer and nearer our own—and whose last dog
cannot be abandoned

without the speed of the others.

The Swiftly Emptying Air

Fields, of starling-rustled
growth,

of pockets
of body-length plants,

in their half-conditioned leaning
at dawn:

we divide their motions and
counter-motions

into un-resolving proofs.

The population-
models

are self-correcting

and the notations, on wind-
charts, are pollens.

Still, it is
almost impossible:

all of this

coupling, and failed-coupling,

against the backdrop

of the symmetry

of half-life.

Capital

Ropes, in the depths of the snowfields,

        thickening with slowly bleeding dye.

        Himalayan cranes landing on the mountainside

to hatch the air-pockets in the avalanche.
This is the birth of the wind.

And the leaflets that are blown off-course are losing meaning.

Along the streets: the stonework is allowed to jewel the graffiti heads:
they are dressing an effigy, mid-air, behind a thin wall of signs.
They are stuffing its pockets

with leaflets.

        With riot-shields distorting the lengths of its legs:
        it seems it will burn for days.

And the heated coins will fall from its hands.
And traitors

will be branded
by picking them up.

Remnants of a Still-life

The table is draped: the velvet takes

imprints of fallen fruit:
and imprints of each,

of her open hands;

     and is that
     a trace of snow—or are fruit-flies

breaking the layer of wax?

And what does their silence mean—
that only certain frequencies

are manned?

And why bind these branches to each other?
Only certain trajectories

flower.

Blizzard

I.

When snow grew too deep for the horses to feed—
I opened scarecrow's shirt.

II.

And in the absence of the Lord
   the apparitions cried—the shades in hell—the backlit gulls on sails;
and when the absence of the Lord, extended to the mind—
   we imagined apparitions—and the apparitions cried.

III.

I remembered
   (by what remnant light?)
the peasants collecting wool from the brambles—and that only, by this memory
   were they required,
to look up from the work.

Salvage-weather

The masts
forest the ice-pack.

There are clothes-patterns on sails.

The nested-goods
formed seals

in the tropics. But here, everything

is scattered.
There are sets,

of empty bowls, decorated with

images
of dogfights.

Everyone assigns the bird, above

the
avalanche,

to cause or effect. They choose a

leader.
They

chart discoveries, in relation to him.

Rising

An old
stylization

of saplings

ascending
into the

crowns

as if
released

from the old

meditation
about the

wind

through the

prayer-
flags

and through

messenger
birds

standing

by the grace
of stiff

paper.

Ascension Theory

Occasionally, a rising whale applies its growing lightness to the air,
and reminds us,

nothing fails its moment;

           images play along a satellite:
           a planet's metallic reflection *(being stripped*

by friction) appears

at the intended speed
and heats at the rate of our calculations

             before flaring at its leading edge
       and sweeping through the instruments;

      fabric,
      smuggled onto unmanned crafts, moves away from our corrections:

so that banking, in any direction,
dresses nothingness

            or veils the face of God
            and drapes

              His moving parts in cloth.

Natural Histories

Origami in aching hands:
twin articulations

of evening;

the pieces of unfinished cross-stitch
of vine-grafts

and figures
wedded by knots in their rings;

the plagues,

among the birds,
of weather that never reaches

the ground;

the relative beauty of looped
transmissions

to their destinations—*instructions*

for materials

that may, or may not, exist:

and new locutions for referencing

sky.

The Tiers of Plains

Newsprint graffiti
on domes of papier-mâché;

songbirds in lower registers:

their neck-feathers
weighted by rain;

the Southern Cross

still fixed
in benediction

of the opposite direction;

the injured animals
whitening the grasses

where they lie:

and scavengers
using these bleached shapes

as memories.

Stained Glass

The beasts of the broken windows using the dark of the church as prey:

        if any of them caves inward—and the others continue
with the dark, it is unholy;

if there is loose glass, in the rendering of the saint, he is trembling;
if there

        is a shard, below his hand, he is asking for their mercy.

In the originals, no beast would reach its saint, but there were weaknesses
where the wind could martyr them;

        and wherever the disciples clasped their hands, in prayer,

Christ hailed them
with fingertips of beveled glass. In the originals, wherever Christ stood,
he was surrounded,

        as in this Gethsemane—where a sword, edged with solder,
        cleaved an ear (and *we* became sinners

abandoning the series

without a window of the healing).

Signal

snow bending ribs of ships from the timber:
leaving

half-hulls
to ferry the emptiness of the clearing

to the
salvage-

crews,

working in teams of two, or three, against
any

other
versions

of recovery: working, in silence, toward their
midday

meal
where

they needn't wonder if there is suffering in
the

next
life

with the fragrant-wood lingering in their
split-

bodied
fish.

Latitude

Stations

in the arctic:
emptied

by auroras:

tech-
nicians spilling

drunkenly,

forward.
With the few,

left standing,

pitched against
the light:

each of them,

forgets
the other's

voice.

The only names

are names

of ships.

Icelandic Summer

I.

We followed a whale, trapped by its shallow breathing against the surface of the sea.

When we returned, we heard the birds giving the Christian dead, pagan names, and said nothing.

It was raining, and beached whales were surviving, all along the coast.

The storm windows we struck, leaned at an angle, against the houses as if to latch them to the ground.

For a week, each dawn was shelved on the slatted shutters of our rooms

and we examined these wooden slides for any disturbances of the sun.

II.

In this quadrant, there were moles, preserved against the permafrost,

being brushed by student-workers;

who trellised the field with stakes and string before they left.

They took plaster trilobites cut from the walls of our houses.

Their empty sieves swung back and forth as if to sort the light.

Interior

The planes,
at the edges of the visions,

piloted, for far too long,
toward the blinding sun

    and orienting your gaze
with the same
coordinates;

and you,
mistaking the sunspots
    for food-drops,

unwilling to lower your eyes,
unwilling

to abandon the vision

whose eclipse
could feed your people.

Instrument

The shrine's skirts brushing the bowls of fruit—sending volleys
of flies into the crowd;

which is surely its teaching on mortality, its worshippers say,
or which is surely its teaching on the winds plaguing the fields—

and it *is* true—that we have worked without the bother of flies
in the stripped fields; that we have
picked, unmolested by bees,

in the barren branches—that what fruit there is, is gathered here,

and gathers flies,

that what river-blindness there is, is found at the shrine—
where your brothers and sisters

are most charitable—where the smell of the abundance of their offerings
bodes well

for those of us falling blind.

As Makers of Sound

Listen
for the laming stone:

a thousand deer
per click.

Repeat after me,

"How lovely—
the snowy calderas:

the surgeons
inhaling,

through masks."

Has someone salved
the newborn's

eyes? Have its
hands begun

to glisten?

Count him
among the rest of us.

Pray,
his blistered lip

cleans his chin.

Firebreak

Swimmers
as studies in low relief

and larvae
cast in foam;

the featherstitch of grass
in wind;

coming undone, again,

as it will;
my disease

designing itself

in you;
replicating

sequences

from which,
you are absent;

(as I have done

with others).

The Continuation of Earth through Light

And the resurrection scenes are stacked to make it seem that the woman is approaching; or to make it seem that her expression is changing; that her anger ebbs and flows; that what she passes, vanishes; and the scenes are stacked to force her left, across the stones, that we might see the Lord; and the woman is mouthing the words, that the scenes are stacked to form; and as you move back, through the scenes, you see that the crowd is gaining (though you pace them), you notice them mouthing the words, repeating the things she has said, *(or had she broken away, to say what she heard)*; it seems unlikely the crowd will part; it seems unlikely their drift will veer; or that she will emerge again except to repeat herself.

Squall

At the edges of the market stalls: a few scales exposed to
snow:

pushing everyone nearer the center;

———

what will we know tomorrow? the anatomy of the beasts
frozen into wallows—imprinted part by part

before the temperature-drop—drafts of Centaurs and Griffins with

wounds where stones fell;

———

hourly,
there are fewer bearings

in the myths—
fewer contrasts between the acts of the gods and our numbed hands—
fewer paths to immortality

involving flame.

Winter Range

The living consent to the living,
and the ability they share.

(The grain is scattered across the woodcuts—

is lying in one direction—
is sanded from the harvest scenes.)

They are chasing the goats

to warm the milk;
they are thinning the pulp for tracing-paper;

and thinking of the places

they have left—*the façade-work,*

of caches in sand,
rising in their absence.

Economy

Gold-leaf figures

       applied to one another:

an accumulation of summer days
strengthening their arms

and their legs.

A few, beveled versions

       of ancients

named for their number of hammer-blows:
"Seventy-three" with its perfect complexion—
"Seventy-four"

         with a flake in its mouth.

And so the winter began.
Hammers continued raining down. Sparks

continued starting

       ornamental fires. Their idle-time

       was spent listening to the forests ring.

And a word for chimes

       needed not exist.

Landscape

After years of raising
the sentinel

> *(with which gestures?)* and calibrating the bottom-wire
> with the antelope:

lowering it field by field until they were gone: there was nothing to startle us
from the loneliness

of being.

The days lengthened. And the blossoms checked the horses.

Rite of Spring

I.

The fox-scented decoys going unfound in the wind: scattering
the nesting fowl: catching their young

in the illusion;

II.

without dust, in the stadium, to dull the steel: the bull is
transfigured:

the idol
appears to its maker: rippling

its gilded back;

III.

and if the wind should seed your neighbor's field
with your own: be joyful,

sayeth the lord,

for he will find you in the clearing, and you will be of little burden.

Supplemental Oxygen

Is *any* exposure safe?

He sends an eyepiece
from each gas-mask
for analysis. But
no one can identify

the strains of the
clouds he encounters
at the peak. On the

mountainsides,
the temperature change
stirs the sibilance
of discarded tanks; and

the steady rain
makes feedbag casts
of horses' heads.

Already, base-camp
has a
satellite image

of the avalanche—of the

miles-wide slab—of the

tectonics

of his

crying too loudly

from the top.

Regents

The fence has been shaking
since the telegraph broke;
nicking your legs; with

bits of telegram
floating in the moving train;

the balloon lifted head height, in wind,
and papers from my shaving caught in the wicker.
I built this to lift the cable.

After riding in his carriage,
his bag echoed in his stethoscope.

I made chairs out of the spokes of his wheels
for all of us.

Come back—
he put away the instruments.
I laid grass across the snare
until it was safe.
I left these nests

a few inches from the ground.

Arctic Snow

Monitoring stations,
on these false-

heights, settling

onto plains of dye;
then through them;

then a season

of reporting on each
other;

of not attending the

distant snows
with any
instrument;

unsure, as we were,
as to which might

offer scale,

to the body
or its failings.

Antigua

The IV warms a tendon
in her elbow, rubs sugar on the bone.

He traces her ribs.
Puts a finger where the robe caves closest to her chest.
Etches a spidery crack on her forehead
            (sugar, the glitter thrown at the skull).

Today, the monitor's tongue is green.
Or it is striking at a green-headed bird
on someone's arm.

Who put so much into that lark bone
we found in the reeds?
Breaks the honeysuckle against her teeth.

Is this the water's edge?
            No, it's a needle.
How will I know?
            It will look like a river.
What if it freezes?
(Puts the machine in the sun to warm her;

a single, frictionless thought
slips through the slack water in her medicine.)

Attending

I hung the origami birds from the window screen
by their beaks

and watched them move behind the glass.
I can imagine the neighbor's fan trained on them

even now. I can imagine you thinking this;
making clicking noises in your head

like the birds when the wind ceased and they touched—
as quiet as the saint, on the card around your neck

dropping the sprig he held, into the reflection
on the surface of the bath.

Then you began typing, or thinking of a seabird
pecking at a scaling knife

and everyone began to hear it
until I mended it.

I listened to the birds chatter from the outside
and checked each beak, silent and jutting

into the dust;
these were your thoughts too,

cutting particles from the simple air.
I might close my eyes now

and meet you beneath the paper birds,
until someone opens the window

and the birds blow back, against the wall
above your head,

like a recording.

New Year

A weeping willow's branches
dangling from a silk screen

over a girl, with a hangnail,
seeking shade;

the screens look tattered where the models
loosened their hair.

This blank screen is a stretcher,
carried through the empty streets

to my door;
I let the neighbors knock
to listen to them building

a guest room for themselves.
I hang a tapestry, I've made
of their arrival

(I tattered their horses' tails
to check the room for drafts)

you are fine
builders, I tell them,
as someone begins knocking on the back door

perhaps, nailing us in.

The Iron Range

When they put a balloon in my heart
I asked them to raise it.
I can't tell

how many times the hummingbird
came to sweet tubes
in the hospital.

Please, don't cut them.
That ticking is my watch.

A boy hung his clothes, from these tubes
and in the pond's reflected birches.
I didn't want to check the decoy tethers.

A clearing in the weeds
where the shadow of a kite lingered;
the calm water in

a font
clogged with fine hair.

Who replaced the diver's gaskets?
A girl with ponytails.

The poor boys on the coast
covered their bodies with black
candle wax, and searched beneath a boat

as dragon-fish on fishing lines
cut through.

One fisherman, thinks the other shaved
over the water.

Estate

Beside the houses:
mounds of charcoal
half-burnt with snowfall.

In the meadow: snow, marbling horsemeat—
there seems to be plenty
in the next life.

Procedure

Who stenciled "Little Boy"?
I want *him*

to make the incision.

"Her feeling her heart falling
is *part*

of the ascension."

If left alone, now, the plaster-
baths

will strengthen themselves.

This
proves strength is not a virtue.

I prefer a taxidermist. Who else
dresses

so many forms with parts?

Sentinel

Its throat turned white
when they threw seed between the soapstone

and I watched a branch dip in the night
as if to put a character on its throat.

Today, they killed the bird

and put a notch
in the windward side of a bamboo stalk

to call to its mate.

I picked a green apple
pricked with a boar's tooth

from the ashes;

each time snow
fills the hole in the apple,

I'll return a tooth

to the body of the boar.
Ahead of me

they are casting teeth,
in the bite marks on their bodies,

with falling snow.

They are cursing at the dogs.

Empire

I.
A man said *the Great Wall is the fourth wall of my home*
and died in bed of cold, with a fire roaring in its draft.

Late springtime, and the birds ate the buds off the firewood cart
as it passed through town.

(What remains of the year?
Only the smell of hairspray, where the taxidermist raised its hackles.)

II.
In Tibet, the air was so thin, a man choked on the bird he pictured,
as he climbed toward an aerie, promised only by cries from above;

where snow shepherds the herds, in and out of the trees.
As he lay there, I asked to visit him.

There is no room in my house,
I shelve flowers on the lily-pads of the pond.

III.
I can see beyond the ships, tilting in the ice of the bay,
fires on shore catching in wind,

as if to draw them forward
into ever-widening circles,

and men in front of each fire, leaving their half-bodies
responsible for what is said.

Self-arrest

I touched a vein of quartzite, in a temple wall,
which had its glacial shadow

beaten back by candles.

When they fell, the glacier fractured the light from their lamps
as if projecting their bodies,

into the layers of ice that hold them.

With sea ice cracking loudly behind them,
dogs set off across the tundra. They carried nothing and were swift.

No memory slowed them.

Afterward, mice scurried into tunnels,
as fragile as the weather,

to connect the intelligence, each man held,
of the avalanche to come;

or is this the connection the rescuer makes,
in his mind,

between their silence and his own,
where he knows, it is almost to think *for* them

to notice the mice.

Moss in the Shape of Boards

I use the scalp of a powdered wig to patch the pommel horse
(onto which he climbs). I feel the bird's featherless body,
beating its absent wings, in his chest. Where are you going, bird?
I'm not sorry to have startled you; into the field, where an ox
lifts its head from the water, with pearls beading on the tips of its horns.
It will not move from you, it is harnessed in the reflection of the bridge,
until its harness breaks in the failing light. It is feeding on the basket,
set in the stream, as I return to an unfinished strand of pearls,
that teething child, hanging by its thread, you ask, *did someone
shoot a dog, with foam on its mouth, only two blocks from the sea?*

You have a scar on your chest. No, it is the back of a buzzard's neck
(staring at my heart). It appeared during surgery. It will not leave.
Its flock has been splintered by the patients in this ward. It cannot
be distracted. The leg of a wading bird, as thin as a switch
of cane, on a monk's back. Now, lower the leg into the water, he is told.
He is learning to lower its legs, one by one, to feel the stream
running through them. Bring me a shorter switch, the master said,
and I felt myself coming closer to the stream. *Why are we fasting?*
So these legs will support us. Practice your breath, before you
shorten the switch, I am told. *What are you doing*, I call to another.

I am balancing until my master returns. *Then, you should know he is dead.*
I will eat until my legs break, and join him downstream. But already, I am lost
in the reeds on my back, I cannot find my legs among them.
You were training to slip your legs between the reeds? When my mother was ill
I crossed the tubes going in and out of her body, until they became too many;
I lay on my side to cover her memory with the reeds on my back.
My sisters may be caught in these tubes, though unattached,
still feeling them, for the warmth of their mother. When we see
through the tubes, that she is taking, more than she is giving,
we know that our mother has fled.

Do you realize we are standing on the same pair of legs? I have not eaten anything for a month, to join you. This is why we shave our heads. We will wait, quietly, for the season to change as we are not sure which head would fish, anyway.

Revolution

I.

A refugee says, *It is autumn, and time to hatch the nits*
left in the blankets, last spring.
A few days later: a hairpin in the side of a louse: *a sign*, they say,
that the suffering will cease.

II.

The traces of a road where laborers spread loads of gravel
thinned with sleet:

I would have thought they were hoping for spring, *but while it was*
cold, they said,
the sleet lightened the work.

III.

When I stopped to admire the farmer's deer, he said, *I only keep them*
in winter, when snow lengthens the fence-posts.

IV.

They said I was a musician, until my parents assured them: *his bow is broken*
and the pony's tail is cropped.

Enlightenment

He traveled beneath the skimming net of the night sky. He let moss
smooth the cedar-root snare.

At the top of a mountain, a god took his beating head for its heart: the lice
no longer controlled his hands—put them on his head and on his crotch;

but I am translating poorly, now, and they are gesturing with their hands;
and by the end of the night, I begin to wonder if they are, who they say they are:

the incarnations of little gods, needing food and money to pass through this world
remembering me; now one of them is laughing, at a moment I do not understand

laughing too hard, I think, for kindness.

Anniversary

After each snowfall, it was as if something had opened the shells,
in the limestone cliffs,

(that we had otherwise forgotten)

and for a moment these half-shells filtered the air
of conversation.

The neighbors grew quieter
as sandstorms thickened the adobe walls,

and I realized
their disembodied voices had answered you for years.

I'm sorry I waited, for them to get sick,
to stand up and point to myself.

But tell me,
if we had lived near a forest

would you have loved my birdsong?

Cartographer's Mood

You left a beautiful body behind
the granary. Morning glory wrapped
around your thigh. So still,
I thought you were in thorns.
Then he shook his crowned head in your mind
and blood trickled from your ear.
Swinging from the wand of a seismograph,
or a bird's broken leg, half-bent nails,
I imagine you climbed the tight loops of string I laid on the map,
your feet covered in powder,
sifting over wet ink.
And he cramped in the third hour
of your meditation, spinning in your mind,
arms out, touching the sides of your brain,
and then he grew a fingernail;
whiskers when you laid him down.
In the fourth hour you were alone, eyes closed,
except for a crow who was using your mind for a body,
and saw the nail holes in my eyes,
you were both holding palm leaves
and they clapped against each other
when he returned; and the fifth hour
was a scepter hitting a soldier's spear.
Then, you said, a morning glory started up the wood
and tore open its flower as fronds on guards
flew in a wind, and back against their thighs.

Observances upon Returning

I.

The bats, in the hold of the ship, crossed back and forth, picking fruit-flies
from above the crates of food,

though only the few, eating lice from the stowaways' hair, would survive.

II.

I remember the wall of your home, casting a bamboo skiff
across the water of the paddy

and freshwater mussels, unable to attach to the mere significance
of the world above, littering the bottom.

With my hemophilia, I needed the water to bear the weight of the leech.

III.

How high were the terrace walls?   The black necked cranes disappeared.

And our children will not believe that they existed here. They will say *surely
you mean the cranes were carved on the temple stairs* (as they were) *and never
made a sound* (as they had) *and this is why you could do nothing to save them:
there was nothing to save.*

And there was some wisdom in this, though it had not come to pass,
and we were happy we had raised such children.

View

When last I took you to the theater, the dogs were fetching balls in propaganda films.
It was springtime and German Shepherds loped past with their ears weighed down by ticks.

On our tour through the Pyrenees, a young ram staggered past with an echo in its ears
(it had won no ewes to hear us) and only in its double vision was what we once felt restored.

On whichever pages I put milkweed leaves I found the never-caving chambers of a heart.
I pressed a corsage here, which made these words appear, as stitching in a paper pattern dress;

but it took a thousand years, for the stalactite to lower one stitch, into the burial shroud;
and leave its tip, where his thought had been, to rise, eventually, into the world again;

you and I were standing on the ground above it, administering thought to the body,
as if, at this moment, the world had not grown from this head, and we could do as we pleased;

the birds were using piercing songs, and had not waited quite as long, to exist
nor visited upon his head, such violence; and while others stood beside us

above stalactites pressing into nothingness, you and I must have guessed
how long the rain would leach the ground of minerals, and force this idea upon him.

Say Feast

I.

There was bleating in the canyons,

        between the herds *(half*

of whom existed) and there were shepherds calling each through the other.

II.

We each, imagined the child, mimicking the other
but as we broke the silence, the *birds* assumed our patterns of speech—

        which were rising,

           over water.

III.

In the sketches Audubon did of himself: he is Mary, of the Annunciation—

        just clear, of the wings in the room.

Brittle Latch

In the reservoir of a lily
a heron drinks the picture water first,
which might have wet the calligrapher's pen.

The first sound was the pulse point
squeezing past his finger.

She checked each, for a place to put the ink
that would press against the page.
Found a young bird
she thought might fall.

Carried code in her knees,
warped receiver bones,
their thread-thin scratches,
the fingernail of a surgeon.

What if I'm allergic to filaments?
          Don't wear a veil.
When did my hands break?
          Those are just slivers from birds.
How will I find you
once the sky gets in?
          Get into the sky
          when the birds quit circling.
Would you change anything?
          I would have grown a blister
          in the desert,
          for something thirsty.
          I would have jumped in a still pool
          to destroy the weather.
And wet the heron's thighs?
          And watch striders
          stitch the pond again.

Lather

I.

I remember the posters of the rebel leaders,

      how the rain pocks their cheeks,

each spring;

   and mud huts, as briefly raised, as splashes in the wallows.

II.

The settlements, truss the ground, we break,

to reach them; and though

    we must expose stairs for the porters,

it is *(briefly)* as it would have been—*the settlements deserted,*
the gazelles

   lost in the shift of consciousness, between rest

   and alarm.

Northern Plains

Imagine the images lost from the walls of snow-caves: do you picture a bird

that portends a dove

being kept for its whiteness? And do you
see a dried-berry

fattening, in its mouth, as the weather warms? Have you let the boy's breath
soften

its composition? Have you watched his father stoke the fire to glaze its eyes—
and to let the likeness of his ancestor

weep? *Yes, the boy is*
beautiful, his father concedes, as he dampens the fire to enamel
the wolves' teeth;

     and when he carves, again, does he lower the caribou's head
to let it feed—or to harden its antlers
in the North wall? And if it still appears too gaunt

will he blow

loose snow against its sides?

Anonymity

The wind

covering the birds in the scripts of their quills
or in perfect semblances of themselves

      and of their flea-thickened thighs; fields,

photographed in hues cast by parachutes,
or in the iridescence of fire shelters—

which inflate in the charred trees
or Westward from the fencerows—
and which contract

      distortions of the birds
in sudden stillness;

         bottles,

in the flotsam-pack, spinning: encrypting the river
we cannot see, and the reflections

      of who had
      and had not

crossed.

Broadcast

Do not harmonize.

Let them think we are more.

Take your food from the center of your field.

If you must speak of the world—speak
indirectly.

"It is a spare flock whose lead-bird has a wheeling tic."

By late summer,
fewer creatures can be carried aloft.

It is fine, then, to avert your eyes.

Pacific Rim

The intensity of the tremors will increase
and the graffiti of half-finished stags—with fissures for legs—will
lengthen their strides.

When we find you, the subtlest part of not feeling your legs will be
the references to your dreams

      as *walking* dreams.
The salve on your eyes will magnify my hands and leave the birds
unchanged.
                            Along the coast, they'll

      use glossy magazines
for the origami of the oil spill.

The statuettes of the patron saints, of earthquakes, will be made on ships. And
even the myths will shift: Echo will have called a

radio show; and everyone with a flag, from Imperial Japan, will call it
"portrait

      of Apollo."

Another Last Transmission

Flight simulations slipping through simulated birds—and through simulations
of the East—extending their reconnaissance

> of themselves—delivering calculations

> for welding the shuttle with the sun;

then simulations of cease-fires—and reparations—and of parliaments seated to address themselves,
or the provinces:

> where open-air theaters filter light by hand: where a boy dangles green-glass bottles
whenever the woman falls ill—and picks the leaves that would darken her child's face: and where

the simulations land themselves—with the boy

> among their estimates.

Allowances

As when fruit trees blot the constellation's head
and loose it—thoughtless and blind—to assemble
itself

in the West;
as when the aviary nets itself, again;
as when they plant a single terrace at a time

to keep from losing light;
as when, under crows,
the shadows totter back and forth

through trash; as when the trash-fires crown
in *December's* trash;
as when astral charts

include rescue flares—and we are, so briefly,
who we are.

Elegy

The dry washes seining the horizon of the horses; men on tarps in the boxcar dark
thinking of Earth, as an artifact of snow;

      the barbed-wire: the near weightlessness of being caught on all three strands
and saying nothing, or calling out;

(nothing, in having knelt, indicating god—and nothing, in his knees never
reaching the ground; nothing indicating prayer—or prayer made discreet by the body)

receipts, from his pockets, lettering fieldstone; and his vertigo tightening the circling
of the hawks—or speeding a thousand years of circles of rock

into breaking, here and there, from the earth: where he is the center of his spinning and then
he is not.

Census

We played a part in a meditation on the world;
we played ourselves, or ourselves in women's clothes;

and everyone cut their speaking parts;

                         the gulls pinned the scattering trash;
or they did not, and it papered the windows, and some of these words
shone through;

we set fires, to recover shuttle-tiles
from the fields—and noted their frequency, on the grid

of shanties—and that the people displaced, with the image dispersed,
were among us, there;

they numbered in the thousands;
until the mourners were replaced—by the image

in the likeness of those

                         who took their heads from their hands.